TODDLER DISCIPLINE:

How To Discipline Your Toddler Without Pressure.

Using Today's Best Strategies, Eliminate Tantrum's and Improve the Behavior of Your Toddler.

For Happy Parents.

© Copyright 2018 by Janet Watson - All rights reserved.

The follow eBook is reproduced below with the goal of providing information that is as accurate and reliable as possible. Regardless, purchasing this eBook can be seen as consent to the fact that both the publisher and the author of this book are in no way experts on the topics discussed within and that any recommendations or suggestions that are made herein are for entertainment purposes only. Professionals should be consulted as needed prior to undertaking any of the actions endorsed herein.

This declaration is deemed fair and valid by both the American Bar Association and the Committee of Publishers Association and is legally binding throughout the United States.

Furthermore, the transmission, duplication or reproduction of any of the following work including specific information will be considered an illegal act irrespective of whether it is done electronically or in print. This extends to creating a secondary or tertiary copy of the work or a recorded copy and is only allowed with express written consent from the Publisher. All additional rights reserved.

The information in the following pages is broadly considered to be a truthful and accurate account of facts and as such any inattention, use or misuse of the information in question by the reader will render any resulting actions solely under their purview. There are no scenarios in which the publisher or the original author of this work can be in any fashion deemed liable for any hardship or damages that may befall them after undertaking information described herein.

Additionally, the information in the following pages is intended only for informational purposes and should thus be thought of as universal. As befitting its nature, it is presented without assurance regarding its prolonged validity or interim quality. Trademarks that are mentioned are done without written consent and can in no way be considered an endorsement from the trademark holder.

Table of Contents

Introduction..6

Chapter 1: Encouraging Your Child to Listen..........8

Chapter 2: Rewarding Good Behavior...................18

Chapter 3: Letting Your Child Help......................29

Chapter 4: Carrot or the Stick?.............................38

Chapter 5: Tantrums..52

Chapter 6: Be the Example..88

Conclusion..103

Introduction

Congratulations and thank you for downloading *Toddler Discipline*.

In this book you will learn proven techniques to prevent tantrums and bad behavior, what to do in the moment when a tantrum is happening, how to deal with bad behavior in public, how to be a great role model for your toddler, and even how to use what you're already doing to make your children want to listen to you. You will learn how to substitute punishments for something that will encourage them to behave and have a longer lasting effect compared to punishments. You will learn simple tactics that will have a huge impact on your toddler's behavior, how to improve the bond between you and your child, along with making you both happier. This book will help you teach your children coping methods to dealing with and preventing anger, along with ways to encourage your children to want to behave and the many ways to use distraction and redirection to prevent tantrums. This book will make you both happier and teach you the most important lesson of all! Parenthood is beautiful, and this book shows you how to open up and let your child teach you just as much as you teach them!

There are a lot of books on this subject so once again thank you for choosing this one!

Chapter 1: Encouraging Your Child to Listen

Many parents can get frustrated when their child misbehaves. A lot of children can be loud, repetitive, and seem needy. But they might seem repetitive because they don't get an answer, instead, they just feel shut down and so they ask more to try again so they can understand. When you are talking to your toddler it's important to make sure they are calm, and you have their full attention. Use short, simple sentences that are easy for them to understand and make sure they comprehend what you are saying. This will be very beneficial to you and your child because they won't ask you the same question multiple times because they received a satisfactory answer that they understood, without you having to repeat yourself over and over again.

It's also important not to overuse the word "no". As stated before, this doesn't give your toddler any sort of answer as to why they can't do something, it just shuts them down. Children can be impulsive and explorative, so boundaries are important and can make everyone feel safer. But sometimes you have to stop them and tell them that certain things are not allowed. The more you use the word no, the less they will hear it. It's hard for toddlers to hear and understand no. The world is new to them and they want to explore all of it. They want to do something and all they know is that you are telling them they can't have it with no explanation or alternative. Hearing no to every question can make them feel frustrated and discouraged. It doesn't help them learn anything because they were rejected, and they don't understand why. Which is why they usually come right back with either the same or very similar question and start to get repetitive. Toddlers are still learning, and they like to push the limits. It's our jobs as parents to teach them and help them understand why we are telling them they aren't allowed to do something. This will keep them from asking the same question because you are answering it and helping them understand so they are less likely to keep asking and move on. Instead of a frustrated, "Get off that!" you can calmly say, "That's not safe, you shouldn't do that because you can get hurt." The outcome will be much better for you and your child because they understand why they're being told to stop and neither one of you becomes upset or frustrated with the situation. We want to give them as much information as possible so they understand why they're being told no and why they aren't allowed to do what they were doing but also keeping it as simple as possible, so they don't become confused and end up still not understanding why they were told no. I am not telling you that you should never tell your toddler no because boundaries are very important and every child needs to have them. There are absolutely times when you should say no and mean it. But the word no should only be used when you really need to use it and you should try to refrain from using it when possible or try to say no in a different way, we will elaborate more on this later. Give other possible solutions other than just shutting them down, this will give them a better understanding along with making your job easier.

The biggest alternative to saying no is redirection. This is a great way to avoid saying no while also moving on from whatever your toddler is wanting to do. If your child wants to do something they aren't allowed to do or currently can't do, give them something that they can do in place of that. When they ask for something they can't have or ask to do something they can't do, first think about what they can do instead. Why will they want to do this? And how can you convince them to get off the topic of what they want? Give them a reason why they can't do the activity they want to do so they understand why you are saying no and tell them you have something even better that will be fun for them to do that you can both enjoy together. For example, if your toddler wants to go play outside, but it's too cold, then tell them it would be too cold to enjoy outside right now but you have a fun, new game that you can play together inside. This way instead of being rejected with no answer, they understand why they can't go outside, and they have something else they can play. They don't have to wonder why they can't go outside, and they will be excited to play a new game with you. This gives them an answer and a positive alternative.

Getting your toddlers to listen to you is not always an easy task. You may feel they are outright ignoring you and that the only way to get them to hear you is to yell louder and louder and repeat yourself 5 times. And even then, they still may not listen. It seems that no matter how loud or how many times you tell them, they still just refuse to listen. It can be really frustrating, even though it's something that most parents deal with. Though it seems that the answer is rather simple. Do the opposite of what you are doing right now. You've told your child over and over to put away their toys? Stop doing that. Children do not respond well to commands being thrown at them and when we go on and on about something they tune us out. So instead we need to make what we are asking short and simple. If you want your child to remember to do something, give them a short and simple reminder. If it's their toys you want them to remember to pick up, then simply just say "toys". It's a simple, gentle reminder that they need to pick up their toys and you would be surprised by how well this simple technique works.

Children learn everything from their parents and it's our jobs to teach them how to listen. We may say something multiple times and then punish them when they don't listen, but this only teaches them that they don't have to listen until we get upset and until they are about to be punished. There are ways to avoid this. One way is to put you and your child on the same level. Either squat down to be eye level with them or pick them up to be level with you. Eye contact is important and forces your child to be face to face with you and listen to you. Next, you need to be very clear and direct and make sure they fully understand what you are asking them. At the same time do not overcomplicate your request. They need to be able to understand what you're asking of them so make sure you also make it short and simple. Follow through with anything you say you are going to do so that you are the example your child needs to follow through with anything you ask them to do.

Keep in mind that toddlers are going through a lot of changes. They are going through the biggest brain development they will experience in their life and from birth until age 3 they produce 700 new neural connections every second. It is no wonder that they have difficulty with their attention span. Not to mention a 2-year old's logic is very different from ours. Most of their behavior comes from the emotional brain, not the logical brain. This is why it may seem like you are having very illogical conversations with your toddler that make no sense. It's because they are having impulsive thoughts that are driven by emotions, and this is the constant state they are in. This is why it's very hard to get an answer out of your toddler when they are upset and crying. Most of the time they have an extreme emotional need to do something that is entirely illogical, and they aren't able to explain their feelings or why they feel that way. It's confusing for them, so they cry. No matter how little sense your toddler is making always try to be understanding and acknowledge their feelings. This is just as confusing for them as it is for us and they have no idea why they have these emotions or how to deal with them. To give you an example of this let's say that your toddler just asked for something to eat. You fix them a snack and when you go to give it to them, they no longer want it. Your first instinct would probably be to ask why they don't want the food anymore. The issue with this question is they don't know. They wanted it, and now they don't. When you ask them questions they don't know the answer to it can make them confused and upset and that's when they start to react emotionally. Instead of asking questions you should meet your child where the emotion is happening and let them know that you understand. When they said they no longer want the snack they just asked for, say that it's okay you can eat it later. Refrain from asking them questions they don't know the answer to as that will just cause more confusion and frustration. It's also important that you allow your child time to process and think about their answer. After they tell you they no longer would like the snack, you should say, "Okay, you don't want the snack. That's okay, you can eat it later." This is confirming that you understand what they just said and what they want and that you are okay with what they said and what they are feeling. And saying you can eat it later indicates that you understand they don't want it now, but you made something for them and they are going to eat it. They don't have to eat it now, but they will at some point eat it. By doing this you avoided your toddler having a meltdown, you didn't have to ask them any confusing questions, they feel understood, and you both came to a conclusion that satisfied both of you.

Even though it may seem like your toddler is ignoring you, that is more than likely not the case. Most of the time we talk to toddlers all wrong and there is a huge miscommunication. We start to yell and repeat ourselves, and they begin to block us out. Or other times they honestly don't understand what we are asking. You may be saying something that makes sense to you but what they took out of it is only part of what you said and now has a whole different meaning. Then it looks like they aren't listening when they thought they were listening, they just didn't get the whole message. Toddlers are young, and they are still learning the language. For example, if you say, "Don't hit that!" they may have only heard, "hit that". Don't automatically assume that they aren't listening just because they aren't doing what you asked. Communication is key.

A great way to make your kids want to listen to you is to make it fun! If they were allowed, they would play games all day. They can't grasp the concept of responsibility yet so it's our job to teach them, but we don't have to make it such a boring task. Play music while you help them pick up, dance while cleaning, sing with them while they take a bath. Children love to have fun with their parents. We often don't have the energy at the end of the day to put the extra effort in, but with tasks that you already have to do, you might as well try to make them fun for you toddler. Do this and you will create a wonderful relationship with them.

Chapter 2: Rewarding Good Behavior

It's easy to point out when your child is misbehaving, but what about when they aren't? When they do listen to you or do something you asked without having to be told. Praising good behavior is just as important as scolding bad behavior. Yet it's something parents seem to forget to do. It's easy to skip over this because we all think that good behavior is to be expected. While good behavior is the goal do not forget that your children, just like all of us, are human. Even adults make mistakes and get in bad moods so it's important to let your child know it's okay to feel angry or upset. When they do, we need to validate their feelings but teach them that they do not have to misbehave and act a certain way because of their feelings. As your child gets older this will get easier as they will learn how to control their emotions. And when they do this it's very important that we let them know that we notice what they're doing, and we can see they are trying. When they see that they get positive feedback from you when they listen it will make them want to continue the good behavior. This is a very simple but effective way to encourage good behavior.

How you react to your toddler's behavior right after they do it will make them much more or less likely to repeat it. If they do something good and get a positive response, chances are they will want to do it again. This goes for bad behavior too. If they get punished for something they did they will understand that is not allowed and won't want to do it again. Or if they aren't punished or get what they want when they act inappropriately that is going to teach them that it's acceptable to act that way. There are many ways to give your children positive feedback when they do something good. It can be as simple as verbally recognizing them and telling them thank you or can be any reward of your choosing. Here are a few examples of ways to reward your toddler for their good behavior.

- Affection
    - Giving your child affection is sometimes the only reward they need. Outwardly showing that you are happy from their behavior and giving them a hug or a high five can be a great way to show you are proud of them.

- Praise
    - A simple thank you and verbally telling your child they did something right is assuring and goes a very long way to make your child feel appreciated.
- Activities
    - You can reward your toddler with either the promise of a fun activity after they have behaved well or surprise them with something fun to do after they have completed a task you asked them to do.
- Reward program
    - You can keep a chart of your toddler's good behavior and have a reward system. When they've done so many good things consistently they can work their way up to a big reward. This will keep them motivated and want to keep behaving well.

No matter what way it is done, what matters is that you are recognizing their good behavior. Any praise should come right after the behavior so that they can associate the praise and the action together.

Rewards and positive feedback are important for toddler's and young children's self-esteem. This is one of the ways they learn what is wrong and what is right. Not only does it increase their self-esteem, but it improves the relationship between you and your toddler. When you reward them it makes them happy, which makes them want to repeat their good behavior which makes you happy. It becomes a cycle and keeps everyone motivated to keep up the good behavior along with creating a great relationship between parent and child.

There are countless books, blogs, and articles of parents warning other parents about using a reward-based system. Warnings dating back to the 1970's that insist using rewards can corrupt your child into only ever behaving well if they think they will get something for it, and even saying it can make your child manipulative. Despite all of this, research shows otherwise. All these accusations against rewards are unwarranted and most of the "dangers" behind them have been greatly misinterpreted. Most of the early studies done on this subject only recorded the evidence of seeing how children react after being rewarded once and seeing what they do the second time without being offered something in exchange.

If you offer someone money to do a task and then the next day, ask to do it for free then, of course, most people would not go for it. Not to mention we don't typically bribe our children with money to get them to do what we ask. A reward can be many things, not just money. Some parents may fear that once they start rewarding their children for good behavior, they won't ever be able to stop. The reason we use rewards is so that when we use them on a regular basis it creates a habit and becomes something you do without realizing it. Even when you know you aren't getting anything in return for it and that is why we use rewards on our children.

It will create a habit for them and eventually they will be nice without you having to tell them or do something without being asked. Then they will start to learn how it feels good to be nice and that will be a reward all on its own. So, for example, if you give your toddler a piece of candy every single time they remember to clean up their toys, at first you are probably going to have to remind them to pick up the toys if they want candy. Then they'll start picking up the toys without you having to ask and then come to you for the candy, and then slowly they'll start forgetting about the candy and just clean up their toys when they are done because that is what they are used to. Keep in mind this is not something that is going to happen in a few days. This is something that is going to take time to become a habit and can take varying lengths of time depending on the child. It could take weeks or even months to no longer need the reward.

Once they do start doing it on their own, you can move onto the next task you would like them to be able to do by themselves like brushing their hair or teeth. Humans do not typically learn by being told something, but we do learn by doing. Once you've done something for so long it will just become a habit for you and feel natural, and that's how it will eventually feel for your children once they get into a routine of a certain behavior. This can include helping with chores, picking up after themselves, or just simply being polite.

Myth:

- Rewards make children selfish
- Rewards make children manipulative
- They won't ever do what you ask without expecting something in return
- Can harm the relationship between parent and child
- When you stop rewarding children they will go back to their old, bad behavior
- Children will be upset when they don't receive praise
- Discourages creativity
- Will influence the quality of their work
- Children will avoid challenges and instead do the minimum that is required

Truth:

- Rewards create a habit
- Rewards encourage good behavior
- They strengthen the parent-child bond
- Makes both the parent and child happy
- Increases your child's self-esteem
- Pushes out bad behavior by replacing it with the good
- Helps your child to feel structured

As you can see, there are many benefits to using rewards with your children. I am not saying by using this you will never have to punish your child but there are alternatives and many steps that you can take to avoid having to go down that road that can be much more beneficial to your toddler and to you.

Praising your toddler and using positive reinforcement is a great way to encourage good behavior that they will repeat and to make their efforts feel appreciated. But there is a wrong way to use this too. Even too much good can still be bad.

The obvious: Too much praise and not enough punishment can make your child expect to be praised all the time and get very upset when they are not praised or when they are punished. Instead of praise making them feel good, they will learn to expect it. Finding the right balance of praise vs. punishment will help to avoid this. Too much punishment without enough praise will make your child feel like they aren't capable of doing anything. It can make them frustrated and feel inadequate. Too much praise can also lessen your credibility so try to avoid overdoing it.

The not so obvious: A study was done on children solving math problems. Half were praised for their intellect; the other half were praised for their efforts. The study found that the children that were praised for their intellect later had trouble accepting failure and criticism. The other half that were praised on their efforts became harder working and more persistent. The purpose of this study is to show that we should praise children for their actions and their efforts rather than something they were given and can't help.

It's important to praise your toddler on what they are doing, not necessarily the outcome. They might make mistakes and not do something perfect every time. But they are trying, and we shouldn't only tell them they are doing a good job when the outcome is what we want. If they are trying to help you clean and accidently spill something you shouldn't punish them for making a mistake. They should be told thank you for trying to help. If they are putting forth an effort then they deserve to feel appreciated, not feel bad because they made a mistake. Children should know it's okay to make mistakes and not feel discouraged from trying to learn something new.

Chapter 3: Letting Your Child Help

Sometimes letting your child help can be hard because you have to walk them through everything and as parents, we end up getting frustrated and just doing it ourselves because it will go faster. Of course, toddlers aren't as good as cleaning up or helping yet. They've had very little if any experience with it and are still learning how to do things. So please, let your child make mistakes! Let them make a mess. Let them drop and spill and mess things up because that's how they learn. Yes, it's temporarily more work for you, but in time they will get better. So, accept that they will have to make mistakes before they learn how to do it right and have fun with it. This will make things easier for you and your toddler. The first time you let your toddler help you with a chore the point isn't to get more cleaning done, it's a learning process. It's to teach your children about responsibilities and to make them capable of doing things on their own. So, let them fill their own cup of juice and spill it all over the floor. Then show them how to clean it up. Let them throw in laundry and show them how you sort the different colors. Let them help you in the garden and let them get dirty. Make their learning experiences fun and memorable. Bond with your child by including them in everything. Don't view it as an extra chore, sit back and relax and just have fun with your child while you watch them learn and experience something new. It's hard in this busy world to have extra time. We try to do everything in a timely fashion, but children aren't on our schedules. They don't understand what it's like to have a project that needs to be turned into work in a day or why you have to rush around all the time. It's hard to find time so it's easier to do the job yourself and get it done. And sometimes we get so used to taking care of everything as parents we think everything is our job and we forget our biggest responsibility. Teaching your children how to be adults one day is your most important responsibility you will ever have. You created a life and it's your job to make them a happy, productive member of society that is a decent human being that will hopefully one day make this world a better place by being in it.

Another great way to include your child in your daily tasks and avoid bad behavior would be using distraction and redirection. By giving your toddler small "jobs" to do they feel like they're being helpful and learning something new while having fun. Distraction and redirection are a long-lived technique used by parents all over the world. It seems simple enough but there is an art to it, perfect it and it can make your job much easier. Distraction and redirection typically work best when you use them together, and sometimes they overlap although they are not quite the same thing. Distraction would be using a toy to get your toddler's attention off another item. Redirection would be giving them something else to do rather than just avoiding the thing you don't want them to do or have. Here is an example of how to use this with your child. If your toddler is starting to get upset, then stop it there by doing something silly and making them laugh. Then redirect them to do something else so they don't go back to whatever was upsetting them. You can do this by giving them a toy, giving them something to do or simply removing them from the previous situation. It might take a little bit of time to practice this technique and learn how to do this and have the outcome you want. Try to catch your child becoming upset as early on as possible. They will be much more susceptible to listening if they aren't in a full-on tantrum. Take a little bit of time to work on this at home and see how your child reacts to you when you try to distract them and change what they are doing. Pay attention to any favorite toys or games they enjoy playing. They will be more likely to accept these when they are in a bad mood.

Including your toddler in your daily activities is a lot more useful than just teaching them how to do chores. Toddlers are creative and everything in life is new to them. They want to explore and learn, and we want them to! But when things stop being fun they can get bored very easily. It's hard to entertain a brain that never stops thinking. It's in their nature to be curious because at this stage in their life they are learning so much in such a small amount of time. So, when that creativity and explorative nature gets cut off toddlers tend to get bored quickly. And when they get bored, they get frustrated and bad behavior can follow. Letting your toddler be a part of everything that you do is a great way for them to not get bored, and to avoid them getting upset by feeling left out. For example, include them in your errands. If you're at the grocery store and they seem to be getting bored let them help.

Hand them boxes to throw in the cart behind them or ask what they think about certain foods and ask them to help you find items. This helps to avoid a crying or upset child in a store and makes the process much more fun for them. In addition, if your children give you a lot of resistance when you bring them along for some errands this can help by making the process much more enjoyable for your toddler and they will slowly start to enjoy it more. Not only will it make your errands easier, but it can make it easier once your back at home. Including your toddlers is keeping them busy and active instead of them sitting and being bored. A long day full of activities is going to build up an appetite and will result in a better night's sleep. So just by letting your children help with your daily activities, this can help them eat better and sleep better too.

Including your toddler in all your activities has so many benefits. Not only does it avoid bad behavior by keeping them entertained, but it also keeps them happy through it all and creates a bond between both of you. A boring trip to the store that you and your toddler are probably dreading can turn into a fun experience for both of you. It shows you that including them isn't only better for them but that any situation can be turned into something fun. Toddlers are happy and creative and view the world as a new, happy place to explore. Adults can get dulled down by everyday life and that's something our kids can give back to us. So please include your toddler in everything that you do and try to see the world through their eyes. While creating a strong relationship with your child allow them to show you the enjoyment you can get out of everyday tasks and you'll be able to see the world as a big, beautiful place just like them.

I recently read a story about a mom and her kids who are a great example of how you can let your kids help and why you should let them help. She says that she makes her kids do more while she does less. This may seem odd at first, but she has a great message to give. She talks about the importance of chores and giving your children responsibility. She suggests that parents severely underestimate what children are capable of. And of course, we aren't going to make our kids do chores so that we don't have to, we are teaching them responsibility. Teaching children how to do chores can be a hassle at first. You must walk them through every part of it and teach them the right way to do things. You'll have to clean up after them a few times and remind them how to do it again more than a few times. But the outcome is well worth it! Her whole message is about giving children responsibility so that one day when they are adults they can take care of themselves. You shouldn't start teaching them how to do things when they come home from college one day and still ask you to do their laundry because they were never taught how.

This is something you need to start now so they can learn and grow up doing chores and develop a habit of doing them. Then later in life doing these chores aren't going to be such a hassle because at this point they've been doing these chores since they were three. As much as you want to make your child happy and take care of them, you are doing them a serious disservice by not making them do things on their own. If they never grow up doing these things, it's going to be much harder for them to do them later in life. You are making things harder on your child by not giving them responsibilities.

Chapter 4: Carrot Or the Stick?

We've already talked about the benefits of rewarding our children. Unfortunately, punishments will be a requirement at some point in time. Nobody wants to punish their child and we'd like to do them as little as possible, but this chapter is going to be all about punishments, punishment vs. praise, and approved and healthy punishments for your toddler.

Probably the most used punishment all parents use is a time out. I'm going to say something that's going to throw you for a loop. Don't use time outs as punishments. I'm not saying to not use time outs, I'm just saying that we are misusing them. The purpose of a time out is to give your toddler some time to be able to work through their emotions and calm down. When you put them in a time out it should not be out of anger, you should remain calm and collected while you do it and you should tell them why you are putting them in a time out. You can simply say, "you are too upset" or "you need to calm down, so I can help you".

Your child should know it's not a punishment and that they should be using this time to calm down so that the problem can be fixed. Or sometimes there is no problem and they are upset and just need time to calm down, that is okay too. Then after they have calmed down that's when you can find out if there is a problem that needs to be fixed, give them any punishments, or find out they just needed to cry out some of their emotions and you can both move on with your day. The purpose of giving a punishment after a time out is because you should both be calm when you give a punishment. They need to understand what they did wrong and why they are being punished.

This also shows them that you aren't just punishing them at the moment because you are mad and teaches them that there are consequences to bad behavior. But punishments may not always be required after a time out. It's one thing to misbehave but feeling upset and crying isn't misbehaving. This only shows that they are now sad. It could be because they are confused, they may have gotten frustrated, and they do not possess the mental maturity to be able to handle it, so they cry. When this happens put them in a time out to calm down, but this does not require any punishment.

One punishment you can do is taking away privileges. If you've offered to take your child to the park after running errands if they behave, and they didn't behave, then you should not take them to the park because they didn't earn it. A lot of parents think once something is mentioned it cannot be taken away. That it would be too cruel to tell them they can go to the park and then not let them. Children must learn rules and consequences. Our whole life we must live by rules, and if they aren't followed we get into trouble.

They need to learn that it's the same for them. If they were misbehaving all day and you still allow them to go to the park what does that teach them?

It teaches them that they can behave however they please and you will allow it. Not only are you allowing it, but you are taking them to do something fun after allowing it. If you've taken all the preventative measures to avoid bad behavior and they are still behaving badly, then that would entail a punishment. It is not mean or cruel, it's giving your toddler boundaries. This will show them that you mean it when you say they won't be allowed to do something if they don't behave. This tactic may not go over very well the first time it's used, but once it is used they will start to understand what their boundaries are and will take you seriously from now on.

Another strategy is to link the punishment to the behavior. This will allow toddlers, especially younger ones, to understand their punishment more and now why they are being punished. They will start to understand the choices they make have an impact and will start to learn that they can choose to do something else, even if it's not the choice they want to make. For example, if they keep leaving a certain toy out, take the toy away for a day and when you give it back explain it will be taken away again if it's left out. That way they are in the moment of having the toy taken away and will associate that feeling with leaving it out. Or if they don't eat their dinner, don't allow them to have dessert. Children should eat healthily and it's important for their growth, so you should make sure they get all the nutrients they need before eating something sweet. If they don't eat what they need then they don't get to eat extras. Doing this will teach them responsibility. They have things they need to do before getting something they want.

Something else you can do is to allow for natural consequences. Sometimes kids can be stubborn, and they don't want to do what you tell them no matter what. Instead of this developing into an argument, if it's not something too important, let them do it. Of course, keep an observation on the situation depending on what it is to make sure there is no danger but let the natural consequences be their punishment. For example, they want to go outside and play. You say okay but notice it's a little chilly outside, so you grab a jacket for them. No matter how much you try they refuse to put it on. If it's not too cold to be dangerous outside, then just let them. If it is too chilly they will eventually want to go inside and put on a jacket and learn that maybe you are right when you try to give them little warnings. So, the next time you say to put on a jacket they will be more likely to listen since they were wrong last time and got cold.

Another good punishment is not necessarily a punishment. It's letting your child make-up for their bad behavior. Toddlers aren't perfect, and they are still learning. They can be forgetful and make mistakes just like we do. When they forget something and make a mistake, giving them a make-up allows them to redo their mistake and try again for a better result the second time.

A lot of parent's final form of punishment would be spanking. This is a very controversial topic because usually, people have very firm beliefs for either side. Here I will elaborate on all the negative effects of spanking.

- Demonstrates that older people have the right to hit younger people

    - This can show your children that older and bigger people have the right to hit anyone that is smaller or younger than they are. You wouldn't want them to demonstrate this with any of their friends, so you shouldn't demonstrate this in your home.

- If you're stronger, you're right

    - When you use a physical punishment, you are showing your child that you can prove you're right because you are bigger and stronger.

- Shows that violence is the answer

    - We don't want our children to be violent. We would even be mad at them if they were violent with someone. If they were playing with another child and that other child took their toy so in return your child hit them because they didn't like what they just did, you would not be happy with them. You would want them to know that's wrong. In their eyes that is what you are doing to them, so they imitate what you are doing. You are showing them if someone does something they don't like, they can hit them and teach them to not do that anymore rather than to voice their thoughts and feelings. Children need to know that violence is not an appropriate way to solve problems. If we want them to know that then we as parents need to send them that message and lead by example.

- Self-esteem
  - Spanking has been proved to be very bad for your child's self-esteem. You are their parent and it can be confusing to them when you use violence as a form of punishment. Parents are supposed to love and

protect their children so in the child's eye they are going to wonder why you are hitting them and not protecting them. It might make them think that something is wrong with them as a reason they deserve to be hit. This can be very damaging for their self-esteem, and a fragile self-esteem can influence the rest of their lives.

- Mental health
    - Multiple studies have linked violence in the form of discipline with a mental health diagnosis later in life. Keep that in mind when you are angry with your child and feel like you want to spank them. One mistake or bad behavior from your child is very temporary but the effects of your punishment can last a lifetime.

- Spanking can ruin your relationship with your child

    o You don't want your child to grow to resent you. When you punish them, they need to understand why, and they shouldn't ever feel like they are being punished out of anger. Punishments are meant to be a lesson to teach your child something. Spanking does not teach them anything other than to have bad feelings towards you and to confuse them as to why you are hitting them.

- Spanking does not influence good behavior

    o You may think that because you are disciplining your child that they are learning not to do a certain thing anymore. But when you spank them instead of making them understand why it's wrong you aren't changing their behavior at all. This only teaches them to fear you and to hide that behavior from you rather than change it.

- Bad behavior
  - Studies have linked spanking to increased aggression, defiance and anti-social behavior.

- Can negatively affect the parent
  - Once you break the touch barrier and you spank your child, this puts you at risk to become an abuser. This may sound ridiculous and you might think you would never do this but it's true. If you're spanking your child, you are doing it because they did something that you saw is bad and you are angry about it. You are striking your child out of anger. When you mix anger and violence you can accidently go too far without meaning to. A spanking fueled by more anger can turn into something else. This can happen because when you feel that anger and

you hit the child that is causing your anger you feel relief. That relief, along with anger at the moment, can drive you to hit your child more frequently and harder each time. That feeling of relief is actually addictive and you will eventually find excuses to hit your child for the smallest infraction. You may think that you will never do that, but the truth is it's a slippery slope that no parent should go down. Especially when there are so many alternatives that have proven benefits compared to spanking. Not to mention that many of the behaviors that toddlers are punished for are ones that they cannot help.

- Spanking is illegal in over 30 countries
    - Although spanking is entirely legal in the U.S, don't you think something that is illegal in so many places might be a bad thing?

As you can see in the argument whether to spank your child or not, there are many reasons to not spank your child. And really no evidence to prove that you should but there are countless reasons and studies showing why you shouldn't. Many people may spank their children because that's how they were raised. Their parents spanked them, along with their parents' parents, and so on. But doing something because our parents' or our grandparents' generation did something does not prove we should still do it. There were many things done by previous generations that would not stand today, so why should spanking?

There are so many alternatives, many that are mentioned in this book, for spanking. Overall, the carrot wins over the stick. Praising and using rewards to influence your child's behavior for the better can have many beneficial effects. When you must use punishment, use any of the alternatives mentioned. When you mix positive reinforcement, non-violent punishments, and give your children the chance to understand why they are being punished, you will have a happy and healthy child who remains disciplined.

Chapter 5:

Tantrums

The thing all parents are trying to avoid, tantrums. Tantrums can be hard to deal with especially if they happen in public. There are lots of ways to avoid tantrums and ways to deal with them when they do happen.

- Giving your child positive attention.
- Give them choices.
- Keep anything they aren't allowed to play with away from them and out of reach. Out of sight, out of mind.
- Know your child's triggers and limits.
- Use distraction/redirection.
- Rephrasing

- Giving your toddler control of some things.
- Keeping your child well rested and well fed.
- Keeping a routine.
- YOU must stay calm.
- Humor.
- Hold your ground.
- Stay consistent with all situations.
- Do not give into demands.
- Teach your child anger control strategies.
- Sign language
- Giving your toddler warnings
- Time out.

Now let me explain and go into more detail about everything listed above. A few things we've already talked about in this book like giving your children positive feedback and positive attention will encourage positive behavior along with giving your child an understanding. They should understand why you categorize certain things as bad behavior and why they are bad. When they have this understanding, it will help them to not have certain behaviors anymore and understand why they should have good behaviors instead.

Give your children choices. This is important for so many reasons. This is one way to rephrase what you're saying. Saying, "are you ready for bed" gives them the ability to say no. Saying, "It's time for bed. Do you want to wear your green or purple pajamas?" insinuates that going to bed is a requirement but gives them a little bit of power over something. This is a great preventative measure to avoid bad behavior. Giving your child options can prevent them from getting more upset. For example, if they are playing with their food and aren't eating, you can tell them to either eat or leave the table. If they continue to play with and not eat their food, then you can gently help them down from the table and put away their food.

The next point is to keep anything you don't want your toddler to play with out of their range. If you don't want them to play with your jewelry, then you need to make sure your jewelry is put away in a spot they cannot reach and cannot see. Anything they find that's new will be turned into a toy, so if that's not what you would like it to be used for then put it in a drawer or a cabinet with child locks, in a room that is gated off, or behind a closed door. Take a second to think about how your house looks to your toddler. Anything that can be opened should have childproof locks on it and any room that is not childproof should be gated off. It would also be a good idea to keep anything they might want to play with not only out of reach but also out of sight. If they see something new they want to play with this could cause them to get upset and cry that they can't reach their new "toy". Toddlers don't understand why everything can't be a toy to them so until they can understand the difference and why they can't play with some things, they should be put away. Not doing this is only going to cause problems for yourself.

A very important point is to know your toddler's limitations. They are children, and they are not always going to be perfect. Even adults aren't going to be in a good mood after a long day, so don't expect your child to be. On a particularly long or stressful day try not to take them into a potentially stressful environment or push them past their limits. You need to pick your battles. On days like these, learn to recognize signs that your child is getting frustrated or irritated and before the tantrum happens put them in a less stressful situation.

We've talked about distraction and redirecting in a previous chapter, but it's worth mentioning again. This is going to be a very useful tool to prevent your child from getting upset. In a short and simple way, explain why they can't do what they're asking, move on without staying on the topic of what they can't do for too long, and offer something else that they can do before they have time to get upset about what they can't do. For an example, if they want to grab your phone and play with it but you don't want them to then you can distract them with something else and then start playing with them before they get too caught up in wanting the phone. Once they set their mind on something it can be very hard to pull them away from it. It's important to not to use this strategy BEFORE they are upset. If you tell them no and say they aren't allowed to play with your phone, then it's already too late to use distraction and redirection because that's what this tactic is used to prevent. You'll have to move on to the next step of techniques that are meant to calm them down.

Rephrasing is a technique you can use with your children where you will change what you're saying by saying something that has the same meaning but a better effect. All that you need do for this is to say all the things that you're already saying, just tweak them a little bit. You can use the same sentence and move around a few words, change your tone of voice, and it can entirely change how you children react to what you're saying.

Children don't always understand things in the way that we mean them. So, we need to make sure we're saying things in a way that they can understand. We also need to say it in a way that makes them want to do what we're asking. For example, instead of saying "We need to get ready for dinner, are you ready for your bath?" you should say "It's time to take your bath so you can be clean for dinner". To add to this you could also say, "It's time to take your bath so you can be clean for dinner, would you like to play with your pink or green rubber ducky?"

You should really try to refrain from asking toddlers questions to something you won't accept no as an answer to. Using this phrasing let's your child know that it's not an option to not take a bath but moves on to what toy do they want to play with and makes them feel like they have a say because they were still asked a question. Children need to feel like they have choice and options but it's important you don't let them think they can say no to things they need to do. For circumstances that aren't up to them do not give them the opportunity to say no. We might ask them a yes or no question with the intent that it's not up for discussion, but this can be confusing to a toddler. When you ask them a yes or no question they think that no is an option.

Focusing on the areas that are requirements, not an option like baths, cleaning their room, naptime, bedtime, etc., something we as parents need to stop doing is asking. Don't ask, tell when it comes to these situations. That doesn't mean we have to go around shouting orders and children aren't allowed to have any input. It is actually very beneficial to everyone to let them choose but give them things to choose from after you tell them what they need to be doing. If their room needs to be cleaned, then it's not an option for it to not be cleaned. Maybe they can choose when they are going to clean it today, or maybe you can split up the work and they can choose what part of the room they want to clean, but they are going to clean the room. Or they need to eat a vegetable with dinner.

They don't get to choose whether they eat a vegetable, but they can choose between broccoli or carrots. Doing this will ensure that your child does what you ask while remaining happy and feeling like they have choices. Nobody, including toddlers, likes to be bossed around all the time. Rephrasing what you're saying can prevent your toddler from getting frustrated that they're being bossed around and can prevent a lot of arguments or disagreements between you and your child.

The next point is giving them some control. Don't let them control every situation but don't bulldoze them with commands either. They aren't always going to be very happy with what you tell them because even though they are young they are still human. Nobody likes being told what to do and to feel like they have no power so don't make your child feel like that. A mistake parents make is asking their children if they want to do something that isn't really a choice. Don't ask them something if you aren't going to accept no as an answer. That's giving them the power to choose something but then taking it away from them. If it is something they have to do, like going to bed, don't ask if they are ready for bed. This is confusing to them because they are going to take the question literally. Let them choose when or how they do it, but not if it will get done. An example of this is something we've previously talked about. Give them options over things that you are okay being under their control but never give them the option to choose to do something that is a requirement.

The next point is an obvious one. Keep your toddler well rested and well fed. Simple enough, right? When they don't get enough sleep or start getting hungry toddlers can become very cranky, very fast. If you notice them becoming irritable, first think if one of those could be the reason for a quick fix before it turns into a full-blown tantrum. There's no reason for both of you to have to go through all of that when it's such an easy fix. Keep an emergency stash in your bag for when you're out and you child gets cranky. Keep some snacks for when they get hungry and keep a few things for their entertainment to distract them from being upset.

To go along with the last paragraph, it's very important to keep a consistent schedule with toddlers. Keeping a schedule will help them be hungry at the same times every day and actually make them tired when it's time to go to bed. Here are a few more benefits to keeping a consistent schedule for your children.

- Healthy play
- More relaxed during "down times"
- Take naps and sleep better at night
- Eat full, healthy meals
- Regular bowel movements
- Gives children a sense of security and comfort
- Creates bonds with parent and child and strengthens values
- Gives the child an understanding of what is important
- Establishes expectations
- Can result in the child feeling confident and independent
- Stress and anxiety in the household are reduced
- Creates healthy habits
- Offers stability when change is inevitable

Here are the downsides to not having a schedule.

- It can make children feel insecure, uncertain, and stressed

- Inconsistent behavior

- Misconduct can result because children don't know what is to be expected from them

- Inconsistencies make it harder for toddlers to thrive

- Children may feel angry, confused and frustrated

As you can see routines are important for children and consistency is very beneficial to them. Routines might include getting ready in the morning, mealtimes, naptimes, bedtimes, bath times, play time, helping with chores, etc. It's recommended that you start your child on a routine as early as possible but if you haven't that's alright. You can start a routine at any time. The most important times you'll need to establish will be bedtimes, mealtimes, naptimes and snack times. These are the most important because whether they are consistent or not will influence how well your child sleeps or eats. Keep in mind creating a new routine for your family takes time for everyone to get used to and you need to do what works best for your family. Be patient at first, it will eventually become second nature to everyone it just takes some time before that's what everyone is used to.

Consistent schedules are crucial to young children, but we also shouldn't forget about the importance of flexibility. If a schedule becomes too strict the benefits will be reduced and anyone in that routine may feel trapped. Spontaneity is also important for toddlers, you just have to blend it in with your routine. For example, if your child is really excited to show you a picture they made but it's time for them to go to bed you shouldn't tell them they can show you in the morning. They aren't going to feel that same excitement if you don't want to see it when they want to show you. A five-minute delay for bedtime is worth it to make your child feel valued.

Next, this is a very important step when you can see your child is starting to get upset. Stay calm!

Children will mimic you and you can't expect them to calm down when you aren't even able to. Studies have shown many people will meet you at your level and feed off your energy. If you walk into the room and start yelling, chances are you are going to upset someone and when they hear you yelling they will follow along and raise their voice to match your level. Same goes for calm behavior. Going into a situation level headed will set the mood for everyone and will give them a chance to stay calm as well. Staying calm is the first step to anything you do. If you are getting frustrated dealing with your toddler's behavior you will never be able to deal with it properly if you don't calm down and collect yourself first. Set the example and they will follow.

Another way to deal with an upset toddler is humor. This is not a full proof method, but sometimes it can completely change you child's mood. Toddlers want to laugh and have fun. Nobody wants to be in a bad mood so try to turn it around before their mood gets too bad with some laughter. It will leave everyone feeling better and let you start over and fix whatever made them upset. Sometimes a sudden change of mood can come as a surprise and leave an opening for their attitude to change. It may not always work out like this, but it is worth a try.

An important step in disciplining your children is holding your ground. This can be hard at times and can be exhausting when your toddler tests their limits. And believe me, they will. It's their way of learning their boundaries and if we don't teach them exactly where those boundaries are then they are going to push their limits every single time. As a parent, it's tough to see your kids cry. We want the best for our children and we want to make them happy. But think about their long-term happiness instead of their short term. It might be easier to give in now and let them do something or have something but that is setting you both up for failure. I

t's not possible for your child to never have bad behavior, but we want to avoid it as much as possible. If your child asks for something and you say no if you don't hold your ground even when they start crying, that is teaching them the way to get what they want is through crying. What you end up teaching them is not only that it doesn't mean anything when you say no but also that crying is how they get their way, and that's not what we want. Holding your ground teaches them that no means no. It's not negotiable and they cannot cry to get what they want.

Referring back to the last paragraph, consistency is key. Even though it seems like your toddler is just trying to push your buttons, they are learning. And if we don't stay consistent then they aren't learning. It's confusing to be allowed to do something one day and not the next. So, when you want to give in remember that it will be beneficial to you and your child to help them understand what is to be expected of them.

Similar to what we just talked about, do not give into demands. Your child does not get to tell you what to do. You are the parent and you make the rules. If you give in now, next time they are going to cry and scream until they get what they want again. Show them that crying is not going to get them anything. If they realize you aren't going to break, then they will eventually learn to stop crying when they want something. But you are going to have to get through the times they do until they learn that. Even giving in once will teach them that if they throw a fit long enough you'll eventually give in. Do not teach them this and do not give them the power to be able to control you.

The next point is to teach your toddler anger control strategies. This is going to be a great way to help them control their anger and helping themselves before they have a tantrum. This will also be a great strategy not just while they're young but will also be the first step in helping them later in life to control bad feelings. An effective strategy to calm kids down is to have them do basic math questions. Although this is a great strategy and proven to be effective, we are dealing with toddlers who aren't quite able to do this yet. We can substitute math for something easier such as reading a book, counting, point to colors and have them name them, sing a song, etc. By helping your toddler deal with bad feelings early on, this will be very helpful to them later in life when they can understand their emotions on a deeper level. It's very important that children learn how to deal with bad feelings. As much as we may want to give our children everything they want and make sure they are always happy, this is an unrealistic goal. Even if you manage to make them happy all the time when they are younger, one day they will have to grow up. If they never learned the skills needed to deal with bad feelings their adult life is going to be very difficult for them. Adult life is going to seem miserable to them if they've never had to deal with any sort of bad feeling before. Don't make you child suffer through this when they're older, instead teach them now so they can become happy, healthy adults. If you truly want them to be happy, you will teach them the tools they will need to do things by themselves.

A popular form of communication that might be easier for your toddler to use is sign language. It can be very frustrating for younger children to try to tell you what they want and not be understood or lack the vocabulary to ask for what they want. Babies can even learn sign language as early as 6 months old, but it may take until they are about 8 or 9 months old. Even if they lack the ability to sign back you can still teach them signs until they get more of their motor skills.

You can do this by signing while you talk and make sure to emphasize and enunciate the words that you are signing and make sure they can see what your hand looks like. You can even let them touch and feel the shape your hand is making while you repeat the word that you're signing. Baby signing experts say this will help any language barrier between you and your child while helping them communicate with you more efficiently and alleviate your toddler's frustration if they can't verbalize their needs. It is thought that children who learn the ability to sign have higher self esteem and improved confidence. Research also shows that signing can help your baby learn to speak using words earlier on. Other benefits of signing include increased communication opportunities, decreased frustration and confusion, decreased caregivers' frustration and confusion, makes pre-verbal communication possible, helps with an understanding of language, and strengthens social and emotional bonds.

A common concern among parents is that their children will use sign language as their primary way of communicating instead of learning how to talk, it proves to be the opposite. It teaches babies and toddlers how language works and works as an aid once they start to talk. All current research shows that sign language facilitates verbal language for children. This is a great way to avoid miscommunication, avoid your toddler getting frustrated when they can't communicate their needs or when they aren't being understood.

Personally, my favorite and also a very effective way to avoid tantrums is giving your child warnings. If their bedtime is in an hour and they are still playing, let them know. Then give them a countdown of when it will be time to stop playing and get ready for bed. Or if they will be going out in public let them know what to expect. This is a huge factor in how your child will act. It's an even bigger help to them when they know what to expect and what's expected of them. Children get very used to their routine and it can set them off when they get ripped out of it. Telling them ahead of time what they'll be doing gives them time to mentally prepare. They can't be upset that they aren't able to play because they never planned on doing so since you told them. If they have a dentist appointment in the morning, tell them the previous day. Let them know how their day is going to look tomorrow. You can tell them you'll get up and have breakfast then leave right after. Let them know if there are toys to play with while they wait. Inform them they can't keep the toys, but they are welcome to play with them every time you go to the dentist. If there isn't anything to play with or you aren't sure, tell your child they can take a few things with them to keep them entertained. Tell them if you will be going straight home after the dentist. Will they have the rest of the day to play? Or are there other errands to run? Try to not have too many back-to-back situations that can be stressful to your toddler. But the most important part is that they will know what to expect. This sounds very simple but it's important they have the time they need to mentally prepare themselves for something that's not a part of their normal, daily routine. So, give them reminders the day before, and give them a few more reminders in the hour leading up to it. This helps them not lose track of time and keep them expecting what they are going to be required to do. Reminders do not always have to be time related, they can have to do with the toys they are playing with, the food they are going to eat, who will be there, anything that you expect out of them is something that you can tell them ahead of time. When you get home from any of these errands make sure you praise them for their good behavior and let them know they did a good job. It's important to let them know when they are doing a good job and just like adults they want to feel like their efforts are appreciated. If bad behavior still did result, try to pinpoint what went wrong and what you can do to avoid this next time. Giving out warnings to your toddler may seem very repetitive, but kids are forgetful and get lost in the moment playing or doing whatever they are currently wrapped up in. And telling your toddler that it's time to do something they weren't prepared to do can definitely trigger a tantrum, and that's what we are trying to avoid.

Even doing everything that's mentioned above, sometimes bad behavior is unavoidable. When worst comes to worst, sometimes there is no fixing the situation. If your toddler is too upset to be able to talk, getting to the point where you can't understand them, or past the point of no return, it's time to hit the reset button. Time outs are sometimes necessary, and they don't have to be viewed as a bad thing. It doesn't have to be punishment, it's giving your toddler the time they need to calm down so that the issue can be fixed. So, when your child starts to get too upset, calmly tell them their behavior is getting out of control and put them in a time out. Put them somewhere they don't have toys or noise to be distracted by. You can start with 15 minutes and add more time if they aren't calmed down yet. If they try to get up continue to keep putting them back until they finally stay. Do not back down when it comes to time outs. This is where they are going to learn that certain behavior is not acceptable and that if they choose to act that way there will be consequences that they will have to deal with. Once they finally do calm down you can start by explaining what they did wrong and what they should do differently next time. Let them know that it's okay if they were feeling angry or upset but that's not how we handle it. Give them acceptable ways to express their anger and how they are feeling.

The first healthy way they can express their feelings would be to use words and talk about it. Try to encourage them to state how they feel instead of acting on how they feel. Always validate your toddler's feelings. It's very important for them to know that it's not a bad thing to have bad feelings. It's not bad to feel anger or sadness, that's something everyone must experience and it's important that they learn how to deal with those bad feelings in a healthy way. There's no reason to make them feel bad for something they feel, only that they understand how to act appropriately on those feelings. And saying how you feel is the first step to dealing with them. In addition to this, you as your toddler's parent need to model what appropriate behavior is. If you yell or curse when you're upset, then it shouldn't be a surprise if your child yells when they feel upset. Or if they repeat things they hear you say it's very confusing when they are only copying your behavior. Toddlers are going to assume everything you say and do is okay and would be okay for them to say or do. So always assume you have someone watching you and never do anything that you wouldn't be okay with your child saying or doing. Sometimes toddlers, especially younger toddlers, will have problems being able to voice what they are feeling. They might not even understand what they are feeling.

Assuming you know why they are mad and how they are currently feeling, you should tell them that what they're feeling is anger, sadness, etc. For example, they aren't allowed to eat cake because they haven't finished their meal. They get mad because they want cake and start crying because that's the only way they know how to deal with how they are feeling or because they don't have the emotional capacity to act any other way yet. In this situation, you will tell them, "You feel angry, and you feel angry because I won't let you have cake."

This won't immediately fix your situation but with younger toddlers, this will help them start to understand what they are feeling. They can recognize their anger, and this is going to give them the ability to change how they react. This might sound overly simplistic, but these are the first steps to teaching your child how to deal with bad feelings and you will start to notice over time them recognizing their emotions. You can even let them look at themselves in the mirror, so they can see what they look like and have a visual to match the emotion. It can also be beneficial to point out other people and their emotions. It's important for children to have an emotional vocabulary and to understand emotions. They should understand their emotions, as well as other people's emotions and this, will help them read a situation more accurately.

Remember that we are dealing with toddlers, as much as we try to teach them all the ways to deal with their feelings they aren't always going to be able to articulate their emotions. They are still going to need ways to express what they are feeling so here is a list of appropriate ways they can do that. You can even make a list of approved ways that are okay for them to express their anger and tell them these are actions replacing inappropriate behavior.

- Running
- Thinking of a peaceful/happy place
- Draw a picture
- Talking about how they feel
- Sing a song
- Listen to music

Encourage your child to choose a method they like and to use that every time they feel angry. But of course, they are not limited to that one option. A lot of books and articles will include an option to "hit a pillow" or something similar. I would suggest to not allow them to do this because toddlers take things very literally. That allows them to associate anger with violence and that they can punch something to get rid of their anger. And that's not something we want to teach our children as an appropriate way to deal with bad feelings. Research shows that when we hit something when we're angry not only does it not make us feel better, but it can possibly make the anger worse and last longer. It's possible for anger to become an addictive feeling.

In the moment in might feel good hit something while you're mad but this is actually training your brain to deal with anger this way. So, if you get mad and hit something, next time you get mad your brain will start to think "hit something". This can also lead to your anger causing you to hit someone instead of just something. This is not what we want to happen to our children so it's important they know how to deal with anger along with you being a good role model when it comes to anger management.

Of course, we don't always have everything available to us or our children that will allow them to deal with their emotions or sometimes they are in a stressful or more stimulated situation than they can handle that pushes them over the edge. Kids aren't perfect and even with every piece of advice you get and no matter how perfect of a parent you are, you will still deal with a tantrum eventually. If worse comes to worse, and your toddler has a breakdown in public, here is what you can do.

- Stay calm
    - If your toddler is going to have any chance of calming down, you first need to stay calm. If you get upset and yell, then that is exactly what they will do. First set the example of good behavior so they can follow.
- Listen
    - Sometimes when toddlers are upset it may be because they aren't being understood and they can't voice their needs. They might also feel like they were being ignored. Take a minute and try to listen to see if there is something they want.

- Keep your voice low and calm
  - Go back to staying calm, make sure your voice stays calm the entire time while talking to your child. It's possible that just your calm voice can soothe them when they're upset.
- Try talking to them
  - If they are still able to talk to you then calmly tell them something that will make them feel better. If they are getting upset because they want to go home, tell them it's almost over and they will be able to go home soon. Do not lie to them but tell them something that will make them happier.
- Try holding them
  - It can make a toddler feel safe and comfortable, even in public. Sometimes they just need to be held and hugged to feel better.

- Do not give in

    - I know this is hard because you want your child to be happy and if you're in public it can be very embarrassing being with a screaming child. Everything you're feeling might be telling you to just give in and give them what they want so they'll stop crying and so the eyes will no longer be on you. But this will ensure that this behavior will continue so as much as you want to, do not give in.

- Try centering

    - This is an ancient visualization technique. It teaches you to focus on this moment here and now, and let the outside world melt away. And letting all negative thoughts and feelings go away with it. This is something anyone, young or old, can do. It may sound too advanced for toddlers but there's a way to make it very simple for them to do and it can really help them at the moment when they are feeling upset. If they are crying you can randomly tell them to focus on something.

It can be the lights above them, their thumb, their bellybutton, anything. It's likely to throw them off guard because it seems like an odd request in the middle of a tantrum. But it can stop their bad behavior and distract them with something to pay attention to and give you a second chance for the situation to play out differently.

- Breathing
    - When your toddler is starting to cry you can ask them to breathe. Deep breathing can feel calming. A way to get them to listen to you when you ask them to breathe is to tell them "breathe in the roses and blow out the birthday cake." This gives them a

visual of what to do and you can act it out to encourage them.

- Time-out
    - Even doing everything listed above cannot ensure that you will be able to stop your toddler's tantrum. Children can get in a mood and won't get out of it until they've had a chance to calm down. If you've exhausted all your options, find a private place that's available to give your child a little bit of time to cool down. You can go out to your car, a bathroom, even a quiet corner if that's all that is available.

Dealing with an upset child in public is hard. Even though it's something that happens to every parent it's also something people can be very judgmental about. When it feels like every eye in the store is on you, it might make you feel embarrassed and people may even make you feel like a bad parent. It's important that you know that even if your child has a tantrum in public that it doesn't make you a bad parent. Every parent in the world has gone through what you did. All we can do is learn from it and do our best to make sure it doesn't happen again.

Remember that certain situations can make your toddler feel more emotionally charged and make it much harder for them to control their already difficult and confusing emotions. People can be judgmental when your child misbehaves in public and can make you feel like less of a parent for your child acting completely normal. Society has very high expectations for children in public and it really isn't fair. Children are expected to be perfectly quiet and parents are supposed to be in charge of every situation. It can seem that children aren't always welcome in every setting especially if they aren't acting a certain way.

Society can tell us as parents that we need to punish our children very harshly and draw a hard line for children acting normal in an emotionally charged situation. You might even say people expect children to act better than adults. How often do adults get away with bad behavior because they are stressed or maybe their day didn't go very well? But how often do we punish children for just being upset? Not to mention toddlers don't have the mental control adults should have dealt with emotions. It is not abnormal to feel stressed in a stressful setting. Even as adults we have a hard time controlling our emotions when we're stressed out. When you take away the emotional maturity to deal with those feelings, of course, there are going to be some breakdowns. You are not the only parent going through this and you will be far from the last.

Some situations like going to doctor appointments, being in a grocery store, or being in any public place that is unfamiliar to them filled with people they don't know, can be too emotionally charged for them. That is why we do everything mentioned to prepare them. It's important to note that although it's good if they aren't threatened by these situations, the goal is not to change how they feel, but how they act. It is impossible to go through life without bad feelings. No matter what your age you will experience bad feelings. The only thing that we can do about them is to not let it affect how we act.

In time our behavior will change our mood for the better. But toddlers don't know that yet and it's our job to teach them. It's very important for them to learn that emotions, good and bad, are a part of life. But that getting through the bad is what makes the good, so good. Not teaching them that life comes with bad is setting them up for failure later in life. It's your job to teach them how to deal with the bad and give them as many tools as possible for them to use when bad things happen. As parents, we want to protect our children and do everything we can for them to give them a happy life but the most helpful thing we can give them is the ability to do it on their own.

Chapter 6: Be the Example

This is the most important chapter. You can do everything mentioned in this book, you can use every parenting tool and tactic available to you but if you are not being the example that you want your toddler to follow then it will never happen. If when you get mad you yell or throw things, then it should come as no surprise if your children cry, yell and throw their toys when they get upset. If you get upset or yell when something frustrates you then you can't expect your children not to have a tantrum every time they don't get what they want. The phrase, "actions speak louder than words" is very true. No matter what you tell them, your children look at you to see how they should act. You are their first example of an adult and what an adult should act like. They grow up to want to be like you and act like you. It's confusing to them when you don't act how you tell them to act because they look up to you and they trust you. Everything that you do, to them, is what they should be doing.

Toddlers are learning about the world and about themselves. Since they don't know who they are yet, so they assume you are what they are going to be. You will be the biggest influence in your child's life. So, do everything that you tell your toddler to do when you're upset. Always try to remain calm even in stressful situations and set good examples instead of bad. If you want your child to eat healthily, you need to eat healthy. If you want them to put down the tablets and phones and pick up a book, then that's exactly what you need to do. Remain calm through everything to allow you to evaluate every situation before acting. You'll find that by working on yourself and improving your behavior, your child's will follow without you ever having to tell them anything.

Children who grow up in positive, healthy homes usually will repeat the positive behavior they have been taught. Children who grow up in a home with happily married parents are more likely to end up in a happy relationship. Parents who have had academic success have children who stay in school longer versus parents who've dropped out of school. Generations of family have even been known to go into the same profession. Such as law enforcement, medicine, teaching, law, etc.

On the flipside, children will often mimic their parents' behavior. Adults who were abused are more likely to abuse their children, and children raised in homes that have experienced domestic violence are more likely to abuse or be abused by their spouse when they get older. Children who grow up in poverty are more likely to drop out of school. A child's home environment has long-term effects on their development, it can even affect their brain. For the better or the worse, children usually grow up to be very similar to their parents. It is all parent's responsibility to make sure their children grow up with a good role model.

Who are role models? A role model is someone who inspires others, through their personal qualities and behaviors. A role model does not have to be a parent, but for a toddler, both of their parents would typically be their first role models. Social scientists say that most childhood learning comes from observation and imitation. Role models can be good or bad, so it's important that children have a good one available. What makes a good role model? A good role model can make a lifelong impression. Whether it's someone you've known since childhood or even someone you met as an adult. They should act in a way that teaches the child to grow up with a good conscience and moral reasoning skills. Someone that can teach the child to grow up and be kind to others. No matter the age, role modeling is a very powerful tool for parents to influence the kind of values your children will have.

Here are a few ways you can be a great role model for your toddler.

- Say what you mean and mean what you say
    - You should never go back on your word, and you should never break a promise. Doing this will teach your

child that your word means something and if you say you will do something they can count on you to do it. This will teach your child to be trustworthy and accountable.

- Set goals

    o Setting goals is the first step to achieving your goals. Making goals, reaching them and then making newer, higher goals is how we keep progressing throughout our lives. This will teach your children the importance of organization, that there is always something to strive for, and to never stop learning.

- Stay positive

    o Your children will follow your lead and see how you react to situations to see how they should act. If you're stressed out, always on edge and unable to calmly deal with difficulties that come your way that's how your children will act. Remember that a positive attitude can change the way you view things and will ultimately make you happier. When things are going wrong it's hard to remain positive but keep in mind you have someone watching your every move. It will be beneficial to your child and make them much happier if they learn that it is possible to stay positive even going through difficult situations.

- Respect
    - It's important that children learn that everyone deserves respect. Ways you can teach them this is by you showing everyone around you respect and also by showing your toddler respect. Some ways to do this would be to act more like a "leader" and less like a "boss". The difference is one leads others by example and respects and listens to their followers. A boss is someone who doesn't do any of the

work and shouts orders at employees and does not respect what their subordinates have to say or any ideas they may have. Yes, you are the parent and you make the rules because you care about your child and want what is best for them but there are ways to do this without making your child feel like they are less. For example; if they ask to do something and your answer is no when they ask why you said no your answer doesn't have to be, "because I said so." Your children should listen to you and respect when you say no, but you can also respect them by giving them an answer as to why they aren't allowed to do something. You should never tell them no to prove that you are the authority figure and you make the rules. This can be looked at as a sign of immaturity and that's not the example you want to give your children.

- Listen
    - Going along with the last section, you can teach your child how to listen by listening to them. When your child is talking to you, really listen to what they are saying and interact with them. Don't interrupt them or try to talk over them. Doing this will teach your child to be respectful when other people are talking and teach them that people shouldn't just talk to hear the sound of their voice. When someone talks, there is purpose behind what they are saying, and it deserves to be heard. Respect and listening can go hand in hand together.
- Relationships
    - The company we keep says a lot about ourselves. Your children should know that it's important to keep good company around. Friends that make

you feel good about yourself, motivate you and make you feel happy when you're with them.

- Self-control

  o Your children are always watching you. How you react to things is how they will learn to react. When you're frustrated and about to burst, remember you have someone to be strong for. Take a deep breath, take a moment to collect yourself, and then deal with whatever needs to be done and show your child that even when you feel like screaming, you don't have to act on any bad feelings. You can go into any situation calm and collected. Keeping a cool head will help you deal with your problems easier too.

- Stay active in the community

  o This will show your child the value of friendship and unity. For example, you could volunteer in your community, sharing your time and talents and meeting new people. When your child gets older this will teach them to be generous and to admire hard work.

- Stay healthy
    - Set the example for your child to stay healthy by eating healthy and exercising regularly. Growing up with this example will help your child later in life. Childhood obesity is a problem and can lead to depression. Be an example for your child so that both of you can be physically and mentally healthy.

Ways to NOT be a role model

- Gossip
    - Never gossip in front of you children. You may not think they are listening, but they probably are. Kids are smart, and they hear everything. They might

misunderstand what you are saying, it may not be appropriate for them to hear, or they might repeat what you say. It's better to avoid it altogether.

- Yell
  - If you yell when you're angry, your children will think it's okay to yell when they are angry too.

- Vent/Complain
  - You should never complain about someone in front of your kids. Especially not your husband/their father.

- Talk about money
  - Kids don't understand money yet and they should not have to worry about anything you can or can't afford. That is giving them unnecessary stress they shouldn't have and make them worry about something they can't help and shouldn't be concerned about.

- Lying
    - Do not tell lies in front of you children. You don't want your kids to lie so they should not learn from you that it's okay. This is giving a very bad example for them to follow. Same goes for secrets. Never keep anything from your spouse and especially don't put the responsibility of keeping that secret on your child.

- Don't make fun
    - You shouldn't make fun of anyone in front of your child. They shouldn't think it's okay to make fun of people. You don't want them to become a bully because you taught them it was okay. You also shouldn't make fun of your child either. Even if you're just playing around, they might take it more serious and not think it's funny.

- Talk badly about yourself

    - Whether it's about your body or how you've been at work lately, you should never let your kids hear you talking bad about yourself. You're their parent and their hero! They don't want you to be sad or talk badly about yourself. This may also cause them to view themselves badly too if they see you do this often.

In short, parenting isn't easy. It's a full-time job with no vacation time, no holidays off and no sick days. You are a responsible for a life 24/7 and how they turn out is completely up to you. Your children totally rely on you for everything. That's a lot of weight to carry on your shoulders. But your love for them is what pushes you through every day and every difficult time. As crazy as it sounds you will miss the craziness one day. One day the house that you can't keep clean and is full of kids running around will be empty and clean.

The beds you want to be made won't be slept in, and there won't be a toy in sight. Enjoy every moment because they are all precious. Even the ones you think are going to drive you mad. Your kids are going to grow up one day and be responsible adults, maybe even with their own kids, living life all on their own. Make sure you can look back fondly on all your memories and think back to all the fun times you had with you children. You don't want to look back with regret and wish you would have done things differently. So next time your children are pushing your buttons and you feel like ripping your hair out, think about how you'd like to remember this moment. Take every opportunity to have fun and create memories. That moment isn't going to last forever, but the memory will.

Conclusion

In conclusion, I hope this book will help you with your toddler. By following the things mentioned, it should bring you and your child closer creating a bond, make both of you happier, give your toddler the tools they need to cope with their emotions, give them healthy ways to deal with anger, and give you the tools needed to deal with anything that comes your way. We've learned how to be a role model for your child, different techniques to deal with bad behavior, the many ways to prevent tantrums from happening, how to turn around any situation into a good one, and what to do at the moment when a tantrum starts to happen. We have learned many different techniques to discipline your toddler.

We've learned ways to encourage them to listen, the many different ways to reward and praise your child and just how much to do it, ways to include your toddler in your day-to-day activities while making it fun for both of you, how to balance praise and punishment, and the dangers of physical punishment. We know now that a huge cause for bad behavior is really just miscommunication. But most of all we've learned that parenthood is beautiful, and you can learn just as much from your kids as they do from you. We've learned that sometimes you should just let go and have fun with your child and experience that wonderful childhood innocence that has the ability to have fun anywhere at any time. We've learned that bad emotions aren't really bad, that it's just part of life. The only thing we can control is how we act. And if you practice what you preach, then your children will have all the tools they need to have a promising future.

www.ingramcontent.com/pod-product-compliance
Lightning Source LLC
Chambersburg PA
CBHW071403080526
44587CB00017B/3169